Drives around
OXFORD

Bryn Frank

MACDONALD PUBLISHERS
EDINBURGH

© Bryn Frank 1983

Published by Macdonald Publishers
Edgefield Road
Loanhead
Midlothian EH20 9SY

ISBN 0 86334 009 1

Cover design by Pat Macdonald
Maps and illustrations by Sue Innes
Cover photograph of Oxford from Boars Hill by
Thomas Photos

Printed by Macdonald Printers (Edinburgh) Ltd
Edgefield Road
Loanhead
Midlothian EH20 9SY

Contents

Introduction

Oxford is a quite exceptional city in its own right, surely one of Europe's 'top ten,' and added to its own charms is the fact that the city lies in the centre of some of southern England's most balmy, unspoilt, history-rich countryside.

To the west lie the Cotswolds, and that alone would justify putting a book of this kind together. But to the north lies rural Northamptonshire, which most Cotswold people would turn their noses up at but which well repays a second glance, and to the east and south are Buckinghamshire, the heady, wind-on-the-heath country of the Berkshire Downs, and the Thames Valley.

Within a radius of say thirty or forty miles at the most is a wealth of lovely places, and the greatest pleasure for the author has been to pinpoint corners of Oxfordshire and the surrounding counties that figure only rarely in guide books.

We have found stately homes that are not in the major league but are probably all the more attractive for that; we have pottered around market towns and tucked-away villages. We have explored country lanes that lead nowhere in particular but, when you get there, make you glad you made the detour. We have tracked down a traditional English Sunday lunch in out-of-the way places that we immediately wanted to tell all our friends about, and we have passed the time of day in the crispy depths of winter with 'real' people who admit they go to ground at the first sign of a tourist invasion, which never happens until May or June, and ends in September or October. So if you can, do your day tripping 'out of season', when the open road really is open.

About half the routes we have covered will take you through the Cotswolds, and the Cotswolds are inevitably the star of this book. Oxford is just far enough from their heart to feel separate, but the city's mellow honey- or butter-coloured stone walls and dreaming spires do make a splendid introduction to what lies to the west.

Every well-trodden tourist destination has two faces. There is the August Bank Holiday Monday face, mucky with choc ices and grinning foolishly for the camera, and the private, more thoughtful face that is closer to its natural expression. Nowhere in Britain is this truer than in the Cotswolds, but it is the private face we looked for.

As far as the other eastern and southerly sides of Oxford are concerned, where Buckingham and Waddesdon and White Horse Hill and Dorchester-on-Thames are to be found, there is not quite the same need to search for the 'real thing'. Just set off in the right direction, with our suggested itineraries beside you, and let us do the rest.

Acknowledgements

The author would like to thank David Wickers for his assistance in the writing of this book.

5 miles

OXFORD

A40

R. Windrush

Witney

Swinbrook

Museum

Minster Lovell

B4047

A40

Burford

Swinbrook

Gt. Barrington

Little Barrington

Windrush

A40

A433

Northleach

Museum

Fossebridge

Coln St Denis

Ablington

Bibury

A429

Compton Abdale

Chedworth

Roman Villa

Withington

B4225

1 Burford–Withington–Chedworth–Bibury (75 miles)

The city of Oxford is so beautifully self-contained that hundreds of thousands of tourists see it and go away happy without realising that the Cotswolds are just on its doorstep. This first tour shows how convenient it is to see some of the best of the Cotswolds from Oxford, using the artery of the A40 Oxford-Cheltenham road to strike deep into their heart while revealing typical but in several instances surprisingly untouristy parts of the region.

Follow signs from the city centre for Cheltenham and Witney (A40). The most convenient way out of the city is along wide and leafy Woodstock Road or Banbury Road – where many college dons and students live – which lead to the ring road from which the A40 is clearly signposted. This route out of Oxford is recommended for tours one to five inclusive.

The first few miles of the A40 are quick, straight and functional rather than beautiful. Look out to the left, after leaving Oxford's outskirts well behind, for heavily wooded low hills rising to nearly five hundred and forty feet above sea level.

Take the turn, after about six miles, just as the A40 opens out into a dual carriageway, for Witney. Not the loveliest of Cotswold towns, being a little dusty and traffic-weary, in almost any other corner of England it would be on the tourist map. Witney is in fact a household name all over Britain for this is an important blanket producing town. It is said that the River Windrush, which runs through the grounds of one of the biggest factories, has special properties that render the

blankets fluffy and white. One small source of pride among
Witney blanket manufacturers is that early this century a
blanket was presented shortly after lunch for the Duke of
Marlborough: it had been made from sheep sheared at eight
in the morning and was a record for the time. Witney's grey
limestone and darker grey thatched houses and shops suggest
easy-on-the-eye towns and villages still to come.

Pick up the A4095 in Witney, signposted Faringdon, then
join the B4047, signposted Minster Lovell. Turn off right at
the first sign for Minster Lovell, then cross an ancient stone
bridge over the River Windrush. Bordered by playing fields,
the river's grassy banks are ideal for picnicking.

Follow the sign marked Church and Hall, drive up a lane
(there is parking just off it) and walk, with more views of the
Windrush curling below, to the romantically ruined Hall. The
ancient hall, or manor house, was built in about 1450 by
William, 7th Lord Lovell, in a rather premature attempt to
create a house that was more domestic than warlike—but he
did not reckon with the Wars of the Roses which led to the
ravage of the countryside. A gruesome tale is associated with
him and the house. He is said to have returned to Minster

Minster Lovell: ruins of the 15th-century house

Lovell as a fugitive after a disastrous war, and to have hidden in a secret compartment in the wall, a hiding place known only to a trusted servant, and accessible only from the outside. But the servant disappeared suddenly, and the earl died, immured, of starvation.

Return downhill to the main street through the village, and continue through it, bearing left near the top of the hill for Swinbrook (two and a half miles). The downhill approach to this tucked-away, mainly traffic-free, pale grey limestone village is a joy, for it is surrounded by rich farmland (in summer, a yellow and green chequerboard, with oak and beech trees for the pieces).

From Swinbrook, you have the best possible approach to the first of the two Cotswold gems on this route — Burford. At right angles along a quiet, tree-lined residential road you approach the small town's main street, a wide boulevard running downhill from the A40 to traffic lights and the narrow end of the road at the bottom of the hill.

Burford is worth a stop, if only for a drink in any one of a handful of inns that were old when Oxfordshire was still a two-day stagecoach journey from London; in one or two cases the inns were built when this was an exceptionally prosperous medieval wool-producing town in the 15th and 16th centuries. The countryside around Burford is now quite bare and windswept, even bleak, but to imagine what the town was like hundreds of years ago, it should be remembered that it was surrounded by thick, in places impenetrable, Wychwood Forest. Early houses were, naturally, built of wood, but then people began to make use of the local stone. Visitors can occasionally join guided tours (on foot) of the town, which are generated by the Burford Society and take place on most summer Sunday afternoons.

From the traffic lights bear left and follow signs for The Barringtons, via Taynton. A 'Great' and a 'Little', so commonly found in juxtaposition, often vary greatly in character, and Great and Little Barrington certainly do. Great Barrington is sad, a little unkempt, needing an extra shop or a pub to inject life into it. Little Barrington involves a small detour: carry on past the right-hand turn for Windrush, past the entrance to Barrington Park, a Palladian house built in about 1737 (not open), then its impressive 20-foot-high Cotswold stone wall, before arriving at Little Barrington, a most unusual village, its houses ranged around a huge, undulating, heavily overgrown stretch of rough ground. Originally a limestone quarry, in summer it is thick with wild flowers and bees.

Leave Little Barrington as if to retrace your route to Great Barrington, but turn left for Windrush. Tidier and smaller than Little Barrington, with a shady copse of trees on the large grassy bank that does for a village green, it lies close to the A40: follow signs for Oxford and Burford. On reaching the busy A40, turn right, following signs for Northleach (five miles). Alas, this potentially charming town suffers from heavy through-traffic, but as a saving grace the church, which faces you on its hill as you approach the town from the east, is famous for its medieval brasses.

More modern, though 'traditional', is the Cotswold Countryside Collection, a rural museum opened only in July 1981. It stands opposite a Little Chef roadhouse at the western end of Northleach.

The main road that still passes right through Northleach was at one time the town's salvation. In the late 17th and 18th centuries it was a toll road, and the revenues from this provided some compensation for the ravages of the Civil War and the vicissitudes of the wool trade.

A few minutes' drive from Northleach, turn left off the A40, following signs for Compton Abdale and Withington. Immediately, you plunge into the depths of that sea of rich green fields and old oak and beech woods seen more distantly from the A40, down a steep hill beyond which flatter country opens out. Withington is impressive, with unexpectedly large, fine houses right by the road. But the ancient-looking Mill Inn is not ancient at all, having been reconstructed from old building materials, some of which came from a disused prison at Northleach, in the late 1960s. The river that flows by it is the Coln, which eventually flows into the Thames near Fairford.

Take the first, much more direct and less meandering of two roads signposted Chedworth Roman Villa — though continuing on to the splendid, tree-shaded church at the far end of the village and then doubling back is worthwhile.

High, sweet-smelling hedgerows, very narrow roads and the feeling that you have reached the back of beyond are pleasant features of the road from Withington to Chedworth Roman Villa (National Trust). The villa's remote and tranquil situation (doubly enhanced by the fact that it lies well off the road) is the main reason it became a comfortable, highly sophisticated country house in about the middle of the 2nd century AD, when life had become comparatively safe and well organised.

It is said the villa was discovered in 1864 by a gamekeeper searching for a lost ferret, and the effect of this locally can be imagined: property values increased, trade for local pubs and shops took an upturn, and Chedworth was suddenly very much on the map.

This was only one of twenty or more such sites in the area, albeit the most impressive: a clear indication that this corner of the country was a desirable place to live. But that was not just due to the pleasant climate (and remember that the weather was warmer than today) but also to the skill and diplomacy of the local people, called the Dobunni. They met and traded with the Romans as soon as they began to invade the south coast, and established a rapport that stood them in good stead.

From Chedworth drive through Fossebridge, then across

the A429, following signs for Bibury. This part of the route
has lots of mossy stone walls, gardens to peep into through
iron gates or rose-covered trellises, eye-catching topiary,
thatched or stone-tiled cottages. In fact, if you go in the
spring, you can see quite legitimately inside the properties, for
local people arrange to put their gardens on public view. It is
an enclosed world, especially at Coln St Denis (the best of it
off the main road) and Ablington. The outskirts of Ablington
lead into Bibury—a tourist honeypot that should be seen, if
possible, on quiet weekday mornings or when all the other
tourists have gone home. Arlington Row, an exceptionally
pretty gabled terrace of weavers' houses (National Trust), is
the village's best-known building, closely followed by The Old
Mill (also open). Both buildings date from the 17th century,
when Bibury was an important horse-racing centre.

The artist-craftsman and visionary William Morris, who
knew his way around hereabouts, always insisted that Bibury
was the prettiest Cotswold village, and if the place has
become slightly twee in recent years that is neither his fault
nor Bibury's. It can be spoilt if you go when everybody else
goes: all those annoying people with their blessed cameras
seem to get in the way of your own shots.

Bibury is eight miles via the A433 from the A40, by which
you can make a quick return to Oxford.

2   Bourton-on-the-Water — Guiting Power — Winchcombe — Broadway (80 miles)

Both this and the following route cover *the heart of the Cotswolds*, and both strike into the countryside westwards from Oxford along the fast A40, then north-westwards from Burford.

From Burford, approximately eighteen miles from Oxford via the A40, follow the A424 from the bottom of the superb High Street in the direction of Stow-on-the-Wold. As you leave Burford, almost immediately the terrain rises quite suddenly and, bordered by drystone walls seemingly badly in need of repair, the road becomes windswept and exposed. This aspect of the Cotswolds is a far cry from cosy villages tucked away among the hills.

Approximately five miles north of Burford, you cross from Oxfordshire into Gloucestershire. Little Rissington RAF station is visible to your left, at the same point. Turn left about a mile into Gloucestershire for Little Rissington and Bourton-on-the-Water. The village of Little Rissington has no great pretentions, and inevitably bows to the bijou superiority of Bourton, but is a genuine and attractive Cotswold community with nothing to detract from the charm of the golden stone cottages.

The road flattens out as you reach Bourton, and you know at once that this is a village proud of its charms because of the way modern houses on the village outskirts are built in limestone — or, to be more exact, have limestone fascias. A large car park (quite expensive, too!) on the outskirts of the large village underlines the way that in high summer this is a tourist honeypot. There is a famous model village at the back of the New Inn, built of stone and showing its age a little.

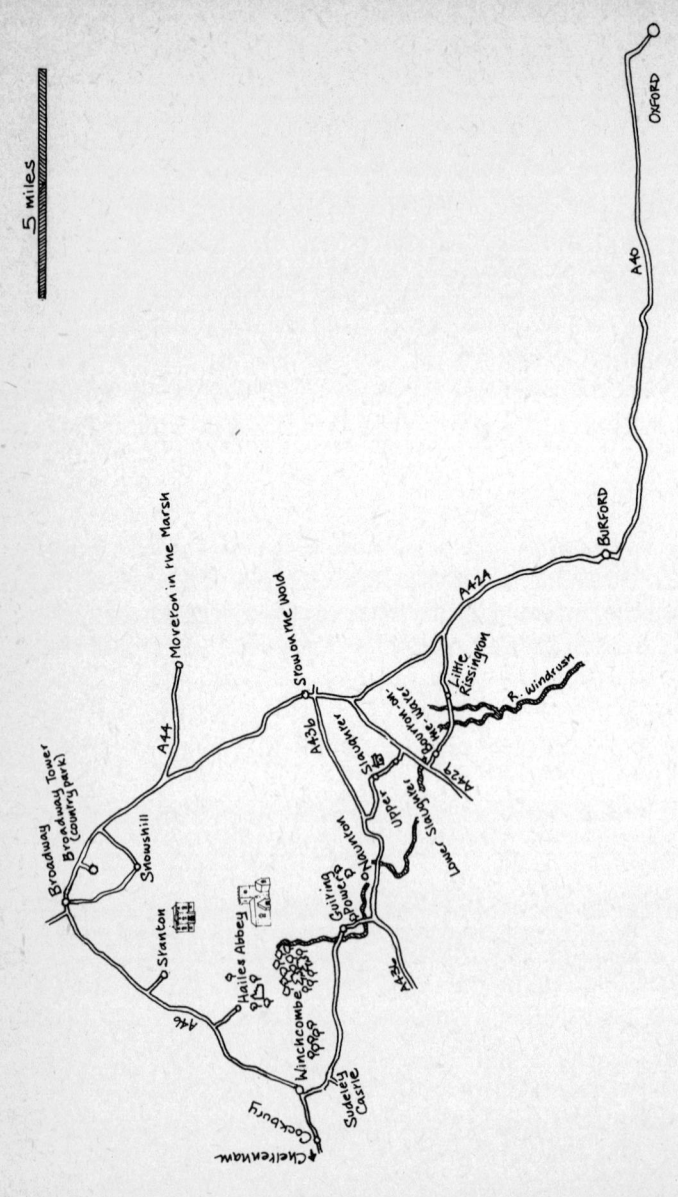

Yes, there *is* a model of the model, and a model of the model of the model!

Bourton would do for people who want to sample the Cotswolds the easy way, with all the assurance of fully-fledged commercial ventures, picture galleries, souvenir shops and several restaurants. Apart from the model village, there is a motor museum, a railway exhibition, a spectacular bird garden, perfumery, and several antique and knick-knack shops. It's a far cry from the wilder heights of the Cotswolds but quite well done in its way. It has been an unashamed policy to concentrate the commercial aspects of Cotswold tourism in one spot, but even so enough remains of the original village to make it appealing. The low stone bridges over the River Windrush—surprisingly wide and fast flowing after rain—add to the scene. There are ducks at all times of the year, and children paddling in the summer months, and the river is bordered by green banks upon which people picnic with impunity.

At the western end of the street turn right on to the A429, going north as for Stow again, and less than two miles along this road turn left for 'the Slaughters'. Nothing to do with murder and mayhem, one theory is that the name derives from a Norman family called de Sloctre. Another is that it comes from the Norman word for 'a muddy pool'. First you come to Lower Slaughter which (perhaps because most people don't bother to continue up the hill) is more famous than Upper Slaughter. Lower Slaughter has a bit of Bourton about it in terms of first impressions: a rushing river, little low stone bridges, occasionally the weekend painter. But here there is no commercialisation, except for the understated but nevertheless impressive three-star Cotswold stone hotel, at the back of which is the parish church with a tower topped by a small spire, half obscured by trees. There are some fine Cotswold stone houses here, with traditional mullioned windows and stone roof slates that harmonise more

Slaughter Brook at Lower Slaughter

effectively than any other type of roofing, as if the buildings were all hewn out of a single piece of stone.

Upper Slaughter is about a mile away, which makes a perfect summer afternoon stroll for the moderately energetic. The road climbs just enough to be increasingly interesting without putting too much of a strain on the calf muscles. The higher you go, the more wooded the countryside becomes, the more panoramic the views.

The Lords of the Manor Hotel at Upper Slaughter is something of a Cotswold landmark, but Upper Slaughter will appeal more to visitors looking for a 'real' community that has made no concessions to tourism, to those who warm to the sight of lines of washing and water butts in cottagey vegetable patches. The squat church is at the highest point of the village which, even though comparatively high-lying, enjoys the protection of the surrounding hills. The 16th-century manor house is well signposted and is open to the public at limited times.

By the notice that identifies the Manor House is a direction sign for Guiting Power and Winchcombe. Guiting Power is five miles, Winchcombe ten. Follow this and then, on reaching the A436 Cheltenham to Stow road, turn left as for Cheltenham along a route that is suddenly more reminiscent of the Sussex downs, being green, rolling and open, than the generally more tightly-knit Cotswolds.

The village of Naunton, straggling along the valley bottom, is clearly visible to the right of this road. It is like a model village used to lend a realistic touch to somebody's railway layout. At the very end of the village is the partly 14th-century church, worth seeing among other details for its highly decorative hassocks. One of Naunton's claims to fame is that the stone roofing tiles of several of the most distinguished Oxford colleges were quarried and processed here. Still on the A436 turn right, still following signs for Guiting Power.

The outskirts of Guiting Power, approached from this direction, are dominated by Guiting Stud – a generous bit of parkland with an impressive lodge and entrance gates and, much of the time, grazing thoroughbreds.

Guiting has a couple of shops, including a post office, a bit of village-green-cum-grassy-verge, some typical small stone cottages, cottages with vegetable gardens. It would not qualify as a tourist mecca but would be our chosen place to buy a few groceries, pass the time of day with the locals, and send a postcard to the folks back home. From Guiting Power drive north-west towards Winchcombe, through a maze of country lanes generally bordered by trees and fertile farmland. This takes one towards a Cotswold high point of nearly one thousand feet, just east of Winchcombe and Sudeley Castle.

The pleasant high road to Winchcombe is characterised by rich red farmland left and right, broken dry stone walls which reach an unusually great height in places, moss- and ivy-covered old stones and lichen-covered trees.

This is, incidentally, the heart of holiday cottage country. There is a concentration (albeit rural and highly civilised) of self-catering complexes, among them the one just a mile west of Winchcombe on the Cheltenham road called Cockbury Court, a 'hamlet' of self-catering cottages grouped around a fine old mansion: a peaceful spot indeed. Here you are close to the highest point in the Cotswolds: Cleeve Hill, 1,082 feet, from which you can see Wales's Black Mountains.

From Cockbury Court it is just a short drive to the outskirts of Cheltenham which, though it is not included in one of our itineraries, makes an alternative destination to Broadway. Cheltenham's outskirts are untidy and unpromising, and the traffic congestion is tedious, but the city centre, especially around Montpellier Gardens and the Promenade, is a fine survivor of the Regency period: beautiful balconies in cast-iron tracery, Ionic pillars, pastel stucco.

Before you reach Winchcombe on the approach from Naunton and Guiting Power you come to one of the entrance gates to Sudeley Castle, where there are also holiday cottages.

Henry VIII's last queen, Katherine Parr, who outlived him, came to live here after his death, married again but died in childbirth. The house is packed with fascinating historical relics, including Charles I's dispatch box. The gardens are superb: lots of yew trees, good views. This is the best way to approach Winchcombe, but as you come up towards the High

Street, which is the main road, there will be much more traffic than one will have experienced for several miles — ever since leaving Bourton, in fact.

From Winchcombe, whose 15th-century church has, incidentally, some delightful gargoyles, it is less than ten miles to Cheltenham going south-westwards on the A46, but our route takes us north-east towards Hailes Abbey.

Hailes Abbey is off to the right, clearly signed, about two miles north of Winchcombe, among much flatter country. Within the broad valley of the young River Windrush (it rarely rushes) the terrain has already lost some of the typical Cotswold character. The abbey was established in 1246, but almost exactly a hundred years later it proved to be right in the path of the Black Death, and three quarters of the monks and lay brothers died. It fell into disrepair after Henry VIII's dissolution of the monasteries in 1539. The golden stone church, half hidden by ancient yew trees, that stands beside the abbey car park is older than the abbey itself. While it is pleasant enough, the most remarkable features are recently restored medieval wall paintings, the best of which illustrates hare coursing, running half the length of the nave, a touching and evocative image that both transcends the passage of 500 years and gives us a glimpse of the past.

From Hailes Abbey we return to the main road (but take the tiny detour to the unspoilt village of Stanton). The great achievement of Stanton is to have retained its character, composed as it is of almost exclusively 16th- and 17th-century stone houses, without having any degree of tweeness. The village street is wide and you are more likely, except on highdays and holidays, to encounter horseriders than drivers. Stanton Court is the most impressive house of them all. Home of Sir Alexander Glen, not much can be seen from the road, but there are holiday cottages in the grounds and attached to the house, and guests have the run of most of the estate.

From Stanton follow signs for Broadway, which is the goal of this itinerary and perhaps the most internationally famous Cotswold village of them all. For some people it is just a little too bijou, and it is hard to imagine real people living here. There, more than in any other place, it is advisable to avoid weekends and summer holidays. A wet Tuesday morning in February would do fine! That way, when traffic is light and fewer crimplene dresses or sheepskin coats crowd the pavements, it is easier to enjoy the great variety of architectural detail in the mainly single-street village. The overall effect of the great diversity is a feeling of great harmony. The Lygon Arms Hotel is one of the most famous in the country and its picture has graced the lid of many a tin of toffees. It is notable among other things for the fact that Oliver Cromwell *and* Charles I both stayed here, albeit at different times.

At the eastern end of the high street you start, almost imperceptibly at first but then quite dramatically, to go uphill. This is Fish Hill, from which on a clear day there are spectacular views to the north over the lush Vale of Evesham. (Near the top of the hill is the entrance to the golf course *and* a driveway that leads towards Dormy House Hotel, a chic, charming, historic hotel — all log fires, chintz, oak panelling, and four-poster beds.)

If Broadway is the main aim, the Broadway Tower Country Park, which you pass on the right as you drive from the top of Fish Hill towards Moreton-in-Marsh on the A44, and the village of Snowshill, make a double bonus.

The Broadway Tower is a landmark for many miles around and it is splendid to discover that not only can you reach it but you can climb it. It stands beside a rolling and attractive country park with a landscaped picnic area, children's playground and nature trail.

From the top of the tower you can once again see all the way to Wales. The 55-foot tower, incidentally, stands on the

Cotswold Way, a long-distance footpath. The folly was built by the Earl of Coventry, as a focal point to look at from his country house, Croom Court, Worcestershire.

The village of Snowshill is pretty enough, with the National Trust's Snowshill Manor. The house is pleasant, but its spectacular contents are what people go for. They were collected by one Charles Wade, who bought and restored the house in the 1920s. As the bizarre collection of bygones and artefacts from all over the world grew — old farm implements and bygones are the more mundane end of the country range — he actually moved into one of the outhouses to make room.

From Snowshill return to Oxford by the A424 (Stow-on-the-Wold and Burford), then due east via the A40.

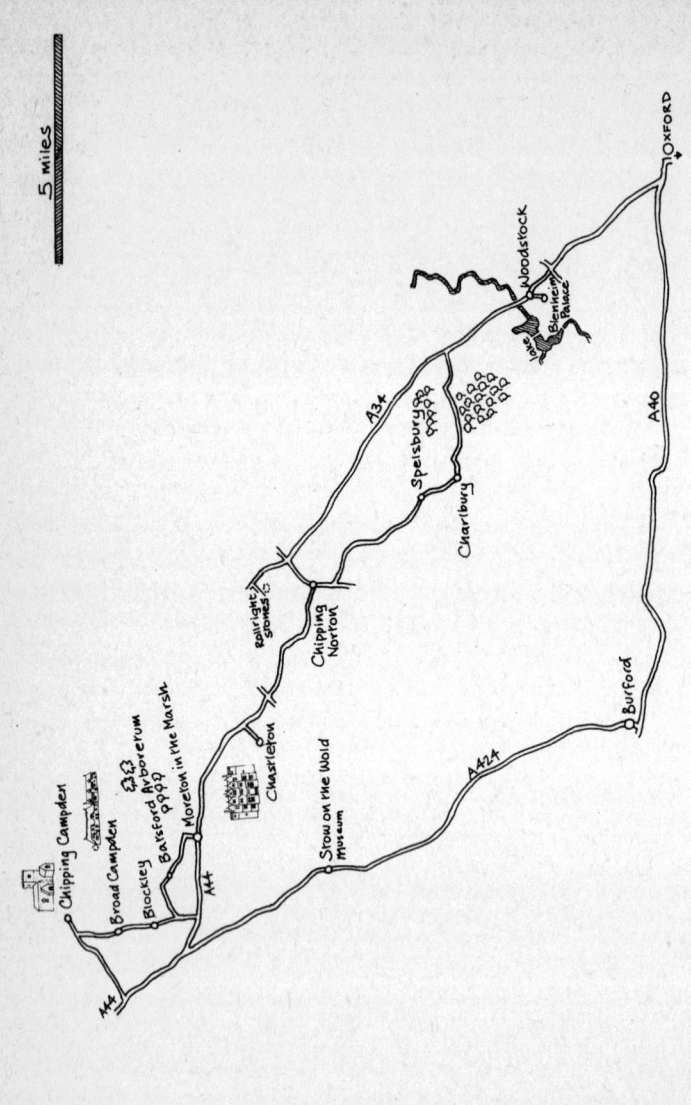

5 miles

Chipping Campden
Broad Campden
Blockley
Batsford Arboretum
Moreton in the Marsh
A44
Charstleton
Stow on the Wold Museum
Rollright Stones
Chipping Norton
A424
A34
Spelsbury
Charlbury
Woodstock
Blenheim Palace
Burford
A40
OXFORD

3 Stow-on-the-Wold — Chipping Campden — Blockley — Blenheim (85 miles)

The second Cotswold-proper itinerary also involves a drive from Oxford to Stow-on-the-Wold.

Don't be deceived, as so many people are here and elsewhere in the county, by the houses on the main road that touches Stow but does not pass through it. (It happens to be the Romans' Foss Way.) There is much more to Stow than this. It has one pleasant and unusual characteristic: the approach from every direction — and no fewer than six roads cross here — is as pretty as the next. There are no fewer than three tea rooms at the last count, a workaday ironmonger's shop, pubs, 'real' shops, hotels. Stow, notwithstanding the considerable charms of Broadway, Chipping Campden, Burford and Bourton, is far and away our favourite Cotswold town. 'Stow-on-the-Wold where the wind blows cold,' they say. Well, it is 1,000 feet above sea level, but you come up to it so gradually that you don't notice the height. The view en route distracts attention from the gradient.

If we had not chosen Oxford as our starting point for our radius of routes, Stow would have made a good touring centre. It is well upholstered with hotels, and pubs which also have accommodation. An oft-quoted statistic about Stow is that in the 17th century up to 20,000 sheep at a time would be on sale in the market place. The historian? None other than Daniel Foe, a soldier in Cromwell's army, who later changed his name to Defoe. Also beloved of guidebook writers is the fact that the last battle of the Civil War was fought here, in 1646, and that 1,600 Royalist soldiers were held after their resounding defeat in the parish church. There is a Civil War museum that commemorates the town's exceptionally chequered history during those confused and dangerous years.

From Stow cross the A429, which runs past the delightful little town (and thus causes some people to miss it altogether) and bear left for Broadway along the A424. Stay on this fast and easy road as far as the junction for Snowshill and Chipping Campden: Snowshill is off to the left, but turn right on the B4081, for Chipping Campden. After about half a mile you pass one of the quarries on the left-hand side which indicate that Cotswold limestone is still very much in business, though for most modern buildings it is only a kind of rendering that gives houses the Cotswold-look. Solid Cotswold stone hewn in chunks is comparatively rare. Similarly most modern and replacement 'stone' roofing tiles are composite. They are clever substitutes, but, unexpectedly, suffer visually from the fact that moss and lichens do not seem to grow on them. As you approach Chipping Campden down the hill, the road is bordered by good, tightly-packed stone walling, you can see the large village laid out below you, and nothing to spoil the view: no ugly modern school buildings, no concrete water towers. A very harmonious impression.

Chipping Campden has had a market since 1180, and 200 years later there appeared the most famous resident of them all, William Grevel. He became the equivalent of a millionaire. There is a memorial to him in Chipping Campden's superb church: 'The flower of the wool merchants of all England'. His grandson was to become a patron and benefactor of William Shakespeare. Several years after Shakespeare's death one Sir Baptist Hicks built the famous covered Market Place (talk about 'those feet in ancient times': the original flooring is pitted and worn and speaks volumes about the mundane history of the place). A Hicks' disciple formed the Campden Trust to preserve the buildings and foster local crafts and traditions that have continued today and help render the village a very lovely place indeed. Chipping (the name means 'market', from the Anglo-Saxon) has its main streets almost completely of stone, much enhanced by intriguing glimpses of courtyards and alleyways seen through archways and gaps in the terraces of houses and shops. There are several small hotels and traditional inns, with a couple of good teashops. There is a Lygon Arms here, as at Broadway, but the oldest inn is the Noel Arms. We have by the way had tasty lunches on more than one occasion at the intimate Island House restaurant.

From Chipping Campden, retrace your steps slightly along Sheep Street, going uphill as if back towards the B4081, but branch left in the direction of Blockley, and Broad Campden. Broad Campden is a much-thatched village with topiary, many mullioned windows, wide and well-tended grass verges, and several of those decorative stone 'mushrooms' that are so popular around here. Towards the end of the straggly village you fork right, uphill, following signs for Blockley. Blockley is interesting because of the number of comparatively modest Victorian cottages and the higgledy-piggledy nature of its layout. Happily for inhabitants and visitors, the main part of the village is on a no-through-road and as in so many Cotswold places you miss a lot if you go racing onwards without time to stand and stare. Blockley is unexpectedly reminiscent of a Devon village for the way it peters out into footpaths, and the way the houses on opposite sides of the single main street almost touch in places. One writer has said of this street that 'it keeps starting and stopping'—an apt description.

From Blockley, follow signs for Moreton-in-Marsh. A mile out of Blockley on the Moreton road, turn left for Batsford, clearly signposted, and Batsford Arboretum (which is only signposted on the days it opens to the public). Batsford is a golden stone village, really hardly more than a hamlet, and is graced by many tall mature trees. The famous Arboretum is open only when the trees and shrubs are at their best, in the spring and summer. You approach the little village, which has many Victorian architectural touches, along a delightful avenue of beech trees: a good beginning for visitors to the Arboretum. The park rises to 800 feet above sea level, and contains around a thousand trees, including a 'handkerchief tree' (of which there are said to be only three or four in the country) and a direct descendant of a mulberry tree in what is claimed to have been Shakespeare's garden in Stratford on Avon. As a child I had a paintbox nearly two feet square, the best of which was the section devoted to greens, around twenty squares, of all possible shades. But Batsford Arboretum in its spring or autumn prime surpasses even that.

Returning back along that little lane from Batsford, turn right for Moreton-in-Marsh. Moreton-in-Marsh is one of the most easterly Cotswold communities, and suffers badly from through traffic on the A44. But the town owes its existence to the road, part of the Foss Way, for a 'new town' was built to serve the needs of travellers on the road in about 1225-45. It is remarkable for the lowness of the buildings. Few are more than two storeys high and as the main street is exceptionally wide, Moreton is refreshingly open-seeming.

From Moreton-in-Marsh, take the A44, marked Oxford, in the direction of Chipping Norton. You cross over the main railway line (Moreton is one of the few Cotswold towns served by the railway). Just a mile out of the town are the impressive modern buildings of the Fire Service College, set well back from the road. Less than a mile beyond there, you pass into Warwickshire, and at this point, you are just six miles from Chipping Norton.

A recommended short detour: at the village of Little Compton, turn right for Chastleton, and after two or three hundred yards, Chastleton House comes into sight ahead and to the left. Chastleton House is unfortunately no longer open to the public, but it is worth a short detour to this spot, for the atmosphere of the place and a look inside the church that stands directly by the almost completely original Jacobean mansion, built between 1603 and 1610. The house faces pleasant pasture-land and a typical Cotswold folly in the form of a stone tower, with an imitation bell tower on top of that. There are still remnants of the once-famous topiary garden, and the church of St Mary the Virgin, which has some very pretty stained glass.

Return to the main road and turn right for Chipping Norton, now less than four miles away. As you approach Chipping Norton, on the outskirts of the town down to your right you see Bliss's Mill. Defying any architectural category, it is more interesting than attractive. It was built in 1746, though most of the present buildings date from a reconstruction of 1872, and still produces high-quality cloth, most of which goes for export.

The Blue Boar was renowned in the 1680s and became a *bona fide* alehouse. But hundreds of years prior to that it had been a travellers' rest and almshouse run by nuns. The White Hart had a later flowering, and was an important coaching stop in the late 18th century. It still contains many good country antiques of the period. There's a nice secondhand bookshop and, interestingly, several good cakeshops. The parish 'wool' church still contains several commemorative brasses.

Four miles north of Chipping, via the B4026 and A34, off our route but worth the detour, are the Rollright Stones, a Bronze Age circle probably dating from 1800-500 BC.

From Chipping Norton follow signs for Charlbury via the A361 and B4026. This road to Charlbury via Spelsbury does not have much of a Cotswold feel, but is green and pleasant, and is a more easy-going alternative to the most direct route back to Oxford via the A34. On a late spring evening I was virtually alone amid parkland dotted with copses and

Blenheim Palace: the bridge over the lake

pheasants. The journey from Charlbury to Woodstock is very pleasant, along roads that are straight enough to make driving easy, but not so straight that they become tedious. Beech trees line the road and although the country is flat, it is wooded and easy on the eye.

Woodstock is not just Blenheim Palace, but a sizeable community in its own right, just eight miles from Oxford, with hotels, probably the best known of which is the Bear, and restaurants. Blenheim Palace is within walking distance of Woodstock's high street but cars are generously catered for on the estate, and the great house is so huge that there is rarely any problems of overcrowding. It is indeed a palace, partly designed by John Vanbrugh, who created the equally massive Castle Howard in Yorkshire, and it is matched by an estate laid out in part by Lancelot 'Capability' Brown. Winston Churchill was born prematurely in one of the rooms: he was to write—'At Blenheim I took two very important decisions—to be born and to marry. I am happily content with the decisions'.

The house dwarfs you—and one might reasonably expect a

duke to be humbled by it. Though perhaps not the Duke of Marlborough for whom Blenheim was created. He defeated Louis XIV's army at Blenheim in 1704, and a grateful nation gave half a million pounds to build a palace. Its interior easily matches its outward grandeur: fabulous tapestries, limewood carvings by Grinling Gibbons, superb paintings, exquisite porcelain.

From Blenheim it is just a few minutes' drive to Oxford via the A34.

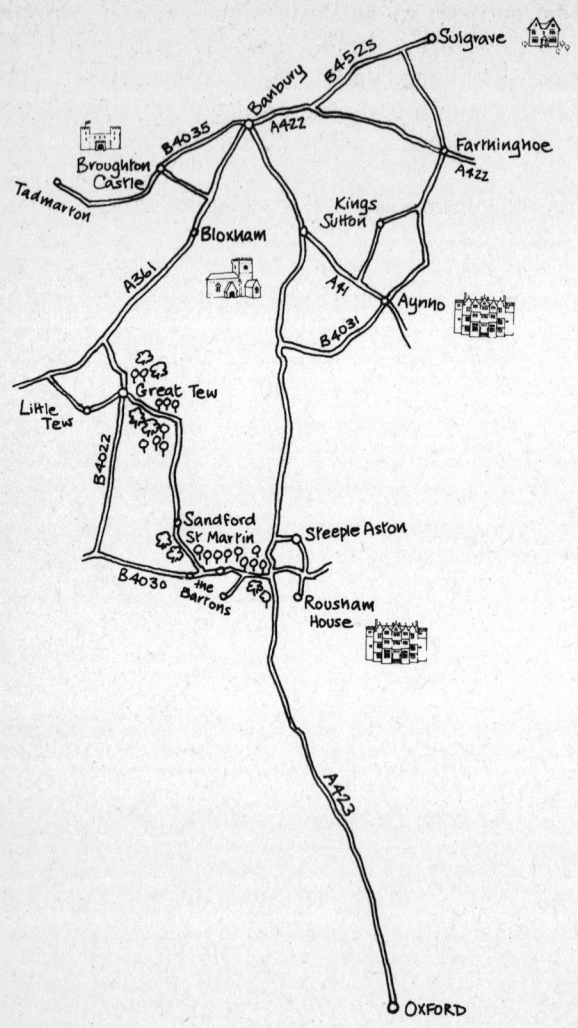

Sulgrave

B4525

Banbury

A422

Farthinghoe

B4035

A422

Broughton Castle

Tadmarton

Kings Sutton

Bloxham

A361

A41

Aynho

B4031

Great Tew

Little Tew

B4022

Sandford St Martin

Steeple Aston

B4030

the Barrons

Rousham House

A423

Oxford

5 miles

4   Great Tew — Broughton — Banbury — Sulgrave — King's Sutton — Aynho (60 miles)

Northamptonshire, whose villages of golden, crumbly ironstone can be even more appealing than the traditional, paler-looking Cotswold ones, is nevertheless one of rural England's best-kept secrets. This tour goes over the Oxfordshire border into the southernmost reaches of Northamptonshire, and its ultimate goal is Sulgrave Manor — ancestral home of the George Washington family. It will entrance connoisseurs of tucked-away, sleepy, utterly rural villages, but we would say it is a *must* for American visitors.

Take the A423 north out of Oxford and follow this functional trunk route, bordered uninspiringly by 1950s and 1960s ribbon development.

As the countryside begins to open out, you pass a turn to the left for Woodstock (see route 3). A comparatively little-known historic house nearby, open to the public as are most of those featured in these itineraries, is Rousham House. Situated close to the village of Steeple Aston, four miles west of Bicester, it is said to be the finest Jacobean house in England. Completed in 1635, the house was a Royalist base during the Civil War. It was extended a century later by the innovative William Kent, who created a few of his favourite features, among them temples and waterfalls.

From Oxford — still on the A423 — turn left on the B4030, signposted Enstone and The Bartons. In keeping with the Northamptonshire flavour of this tour, as you approach the village sign for The Bartons — actually three villages, Steeple Barton, Westcott Barton and Middle Barton — you will see a gatehouse on the left of the road built of rich yellow ironstone that is typical of the best of Northamptonshire.

As you leave Middle Barton behind, take the right turn, marked Sandford St Martin (three miles) and Great Tew (three and a half miles). Now the trees that decorated the landscape between the A423 and The Bartons come right up to the road, and form a cathedral roof of beech and chestnut boughs, set off by wide grassy roadside verges. (Horse chestnuts actually do have an equine connection: they used to be fed to horses with breathing difficulties.)

Sandford is very pretty, a long and harmonious brick village whose only street reveals a second vista of delightful architectural cameos when it bends (by a fine original market cross of about 1500). There are several fine houses by the road — nicely mixed with modest, rose-covered cottages — and even finer ones we can only guess at from their tree-lined drives leading off the main street.

A couple of hundred yards beyond Sandford, turn sharp left at the sign for Great Tew (one mile) and Little Tew (two miles), and thus along increasingly leafy, intriguingly dark and overgrown lanes into one of Oxfordshire's hidden treasures.

Even Great Tew's telephone box is painted grey: it was obviously felt that bright red would not be in keeping with the scattered, often half-overgrown, picturesquely thatched cottages. It is the kind of place, sadly neglected in parts and much in need of sympathetic restoration, where cats doze in the middle of the road and cyclists rest up and investigate their lunchtime sandwiches. The village has been known for its oppressive or neglectful landlords. One of them, Sir Lawrence Tanfield, suffered the indignity of having a petition against him presented at the House of Lords in 1624, for arbitrarily enclosing seven acres of the village's best pasture and for not paying his dues to the parish church.

Follow signs from Great Tew for Little Tew and join the B4022, going north. Turn right on reaching the A361, towards Bloxham, the 198-foot spire of whose church is

Thatched cottages at Great Tew

clearly visible on your right as you pass through the village. It is a great local landmark; its soft, orange stone, probably quarried in Warwickshire, enabled the stonemasons to carve it finely, but also allows the weather to eat it away. The east window was designed by two Cotswolds aficionados, William Morris and Edward Burne-Jones. Bloxham school, whose many-storeyed building dominates the northern end of the small town, is a minor public school established in 1860.

Turn left for Tadmarton as you leave the outskirts of Bloxham, then right on reaching the B4035. Once on this road, you should be able to pick out the imposing Broughton Castle through the trees, away to the left. Reached by a narrow lane to the (sharp) left of the B4035, it is surrounded by an impressive, deep moat famous for its waterlilies. It has been the home of the Fiennes family — pronounced Fines — for over five hundred years, perhaps the most famous of whom was Celia Fiennes, the 17th-century travel writer. About twenty thousand people visit Broughton every year, and although it is not spectacular, it has a moat, a good helping of battlements, and quite a following among film and TV commercial producers searching for authentic-looking locations. Broughton figured large, for example, in 'Joseph Andrews' and 'The Slipper and the Rose'. It is a lived-in place, the home of Lord and Lady Saye and Sele, where home-made cream teas are a speciality when the castle is open.

From Broughton it is two miles on the B4035 to Banbury, which is probably best known for its cross: 'Ride a cock horse to Banbury Cross / To see a fine lady upon a white horse / Rings on her fingers, bells on her toes / She shall have music wherever she goes'.

It is believed that the 'fine lady' was a member of the Fiennes family. Cromwell's faction, who were favoured by the Fiennes, are said to have pulled down the original cross during the Civil War, and today's is a Victorian replica. Banbury is a crossroads of four major trunk roads and, it seems, always busy. The best of the town, including an open market nicely co-existing with more permanent shops, lies at the centre of a spider's web of ring roads. There are several good bakers and pastry shops, which is just as well because people still stop here to buy the famous Banbury cakes, which are flaky pastry cases coated with sugar and filled with currants. Unaccompanied, perhaps on the dry side; best when washed down with cups of tea.

Follow signs for Brackley (A4525); about two miles out of the town you cross into Northamptonshire, then, less than a mile beyond, take the left fork signposted Northampton (B4525). The northern outskirts of Banbury are not very pretty, and contrast greatly with views from this well-surfaced, pleasantly undulating road as you leave the town. Quite quickly you are just high enough to vouchsafe panoramic views over surrounding farms and woods — a classic pattern of greens, yellows and browns.

Take the unclassified road marked Sulgrave off the B4525. Sulgrave promises a lot as you approach it: thatched, dark grey stone houses, half hidden by tall trees, and a glimpse of a church tower. The best of it, however, is around Sulgrave Manor itself, which you reach by taking the first (unsignposted) left fork as you reach the village.

The wide village lanes snaking away from Sulgrave Manor may tempt you to stroll, and if you follow them you will have a long, entirely rural walk round the furthest extremes of the village before coming back to your point of departure. Sulgrave Manor was the home of Lawrence Washington (an ancestor of George Washington), a prosperous Northampton wool merchant who bought the estate in 1537. It was his great-grandson who emigrated to Virginia and started the American line of the family.

The house, part Elizabethan, part Queen Anne, is a delight, its interior especially remarkable for the collection of unusual antique furniture. Among the details that help so much to recapture the past are a dolls' tea set of over 60 pieces and a fourposter bed hung with drapes decorated with original Elizabethan embroidery.

From Sulgrave, you return to Oxford, but via two outstandingly interesting villages. Return to the B4525 but at the crossroads fork left (signed Marston St Lawrence), then follow signs for Farthinghoe (the best of which, worth seeing, lies off the road). Then head for Aynho, turning sharp right when you come to a sign for King's Sutton. This is one of Northamptonshire's prettiest villages, the spire of whose parish church, at the western end, is a famous local landmark. By coincidence, it is precisely the same height, at 198 feet, as Bloxham's. This large village might have become a fashionable spa, like Cheltenham or Buxton, when in the 18th century health-giving water was discovered, but it remained a backwater, with a charming green by the church.

From King's Sutton follow signs for Aynho (two and a half miles), turning left on reaching the A41 Bicester road. Though it suffers from heavy traffic, Aynho is good to look at: the Cartwright Arms is a fine old coaching inn of the

smaller rural sort, and in summer the stone cottages—
including new ones that blend well—are covered in rambling
roses. Several also have apricot trees, the fruit of which was
once used to pay church tithes. Aynhoe Park, home of the
Cartwrights for 350 years, was, like Broughton Castle, a
Cromwellian stronghold in the Civil War. It is an elegant
17th-century mansion, the exterior of which is seen at its best
from the main road.

From Aynho, take the A41 as far as the junction with the
A43, and take the A43 to Oxford—approximately 20 miles.

5   Bicester — Buckingham — Claydon House — Waddesdon Manor (80 miles)

This route takes you, again via north Oxford, into rural Buckinghamshire and to a couple of stately homes that are not perhaps in the major league but are nonetheless delightful. The journey is not remarkable for the countryside you pass through (the Cotswolds-proper, after all, are a hard act to follow), and it is what lies between stretches of unexciting, if pleasant, farmland that makes it worthwhile.

Follow signs for Bicester, first via the A43 Northampton road, then via the A421 to Bicester and Buckingham. The A421 branches off from the A43 near Weston-on-the-Green, a village that would be much prettier if it were not for the thunderous through-traffic. The best of Weston is to be found at the historic Weston Manor Hotel, quietly set well back from the road. It is popular with Oxford people, being just far enough from the city (about eight miles) to make a pleasant gastronomic excursion. And the dining room here has a minstrels' gallery, which adds atmosphere.

Though one does not cross it, the flat, barren-looking stretch of land to the right of the road is Otmoor. The planned extension of the M40 motorway across Otmoor caused a lot of controversy in 1982 and beyond, many local people feeling that this lonely belt of marshland — one of the few remaining wildernesses in the south of England — should be left to its own mysterious devices.

To reach Bicester along the fast and easy A421 is a quick and easy matter, and many north Oxford families prefer to do their Saturday afternoon shopping here. This ancient market town has managed to preserve the width of its main streets and the openness of its market square, and even the familiar

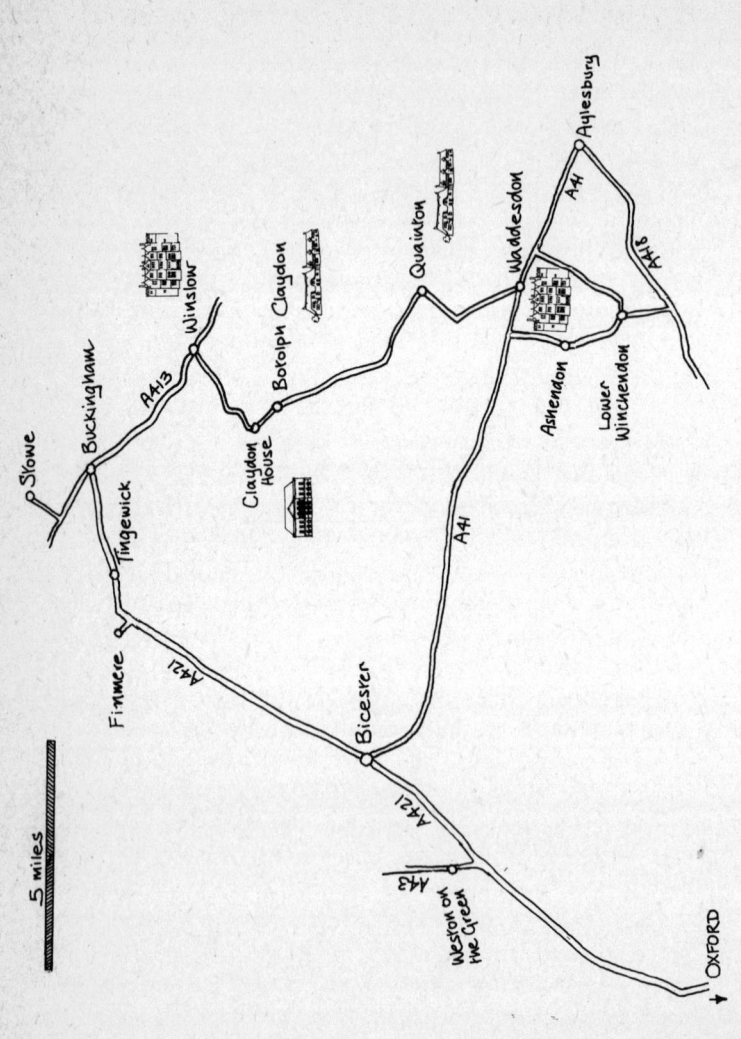

chain stores are set off to the best advantage. Until the 1930s they used occasionally to roast whole oxen in the market square, employing an experienced ox-roaster from Stratford-upon-Avon, to raise funds for local causes. Less palatable are the foxes that have been hunted hereabouts by the local hunt, which was founded in about 1700 — one of the oldest in the country.

The RAF station, which we pass immediately north of Bicester en route for Buckingham, is actually an ordnance depot responsible for kitting out British servicemen.

The A421 runs north-east as far as Finmere, then bears sharply right into Tingewick, to the east, en route for Buckingham. At Finmere there is a huge, sprawling local-authority-approved open-air Sunday market. There is, incidentally, a sign directing people to Claydon House between Bicester and Tingewick, but on this route you approach the mansion from a different direction.

Buckingham is assumed by many casual visitors to be the county town of Buckinghamshire, though it has been denied that privilege ever since 1725, when a fire destroyed virtually all the town and administration was removed to Aylesbury. So nearly all the town we see today was built shortly after 1725, and it has a slightly faded Georgian elegance that casts quite a spell. On the Bicester side of Buckingham are two or three antique shops with middle-of-the-road goods at reasonable prices. Not much in the way of elegant Chippendale, perhaps, but we have spotted some good pieces of Victoriana and interesting bygones.

Until the end of 1982 we would have added a note of caution about horrific traffic conditions in Buckingham, which was at the mercy of several major roads converging in the town centre. Happily, there is now a bypass for most routes, and the town centre is used mainly by local traffic.

From Buckingham there is a worthwhile detour if time permits. This is via Silverstone, on the A422, then an unclassified road to Stowe School, one of only a few major public schools in the country whose grounds are open to the public. John Vanbrugh, Robert Adam, Capability Brown and William Kent all had a hand in the creation of the gardens, which could be considered the best example of 18th-century classically-inspired garden designs in Britain: there are grottoes, temples, lakes, and a famous covered bridge. The village was moved, in 1713, to make way for the estate, and the 13th-century church is all that remains of it.

From Buckingham take the A413 Aylesbury road as far as Winslow. To get to Winslow Hall, at the eastern end of the small town and one reason for seeing this unassuming little place, go right along the high street, and stay on the main road as it bears to the left. The imposing red brick mansion is thought to have been designed by Christopher Wren and completed in about 1700, though all that is known for sure is that Wren (busy on the completion of the new St Paul's Cathedral) checked the accounts. Winslow is a 'coaching inn' kind of place, with a good selection of pubs of character: a general ironmonger's, a low-ceilinged off-licence, an upmarket delicatessen (Epicure tinned fruit, jars of *marrons glacés*). The best place for parking is the market square, if there is room: by the same law of nature that dictates that bread and butter always falls butter side first, somebody usually gets the last parking space just ahead of you.

From the high street follow signs for Verney Junction and The Claydons. As you approach Verney Junction you will have the embankment of the Oxford to Bletchley railway to your left, but you will try in vain to spot any kind of railway junction at Verney: the Aylesbury to Buckingham branch line that used to cross here is long closed. There is no village to speak of here, and the name Verney actually perpetuates that of Sir Harry Verney of Claydon House, who was a landowner and chairman of the Aylesbury and Buckingham Railway. There is an attractive 'village' pub, however, worth a stop in which, perhaps, to savour the rather pleasant forlornness of the place.

From Verney follow signs for Middle Claydon, en route for which lies Claydon House. On its slight hill, half surrounded by tall trees and enhanced by an impressive stable block and a church tower hard by, it promises a lot, and you will not be disappointed: the interior is spectacular, a lovely example of no-expense-spared Georgian elegance, and the park is exquisite: there is a serpentine lake below the house, and sweeping views to the south. Sir Harry Verney, incidentally, married Florence Nightingale's sister and that famous lady lived at Claydon during the last few years of her life. Her bedroom is accessible to visitors.

Instead of retracing your route, it is preferable on leaving Claydon House to turn left at the exit and follow the road round the estate to Botolph Claydon — a village that, unusually, has lots of thatched roofs topping cottages of red brick or black and white half timbering. Beyond Botolph Claydon, follow signs for Quainton, en route for Waddesdon.

Quainton, amid rather scrubby, lightly wooded, heavily farmed countryside straddled by 33,000-volt electricity pylons, overcomes its bland surroundings. It is one of Buckinghamshire's prettiest villages, with enough remaining of its 18th-century heyday to make a stop worthwhile. The original market cross still stands, there's a windmill that is open occasionally to the public, a row of elegant Tudor almshouses standing next to the tree-shadowed parish church, a triangular village green.

Quainton's most famous character was George Lipscomb, who devoted his life to a history of the county. He never saw this completed, and died penniless in London — only just saved from debtors' prison by the intervention of friends — in 1846. There used to be quite a network of railway lines hereabouts, but all that remains near Quainton is three-

The Almshouses and Parish Church at Quainton

quarters of a mile of track, now cared for by the Quainton Railway Society, on which steam trains shuttle to and fro on summer Sunday mornings.

The approach to Waddesdon does not promise well, from this or any other direction, but the main street of this largely purpose-built village has lots of charm, and builds one's expectations of the fabulous country home of the Rothschild family. Many buildings in the village date from the 1880s, after Waddesdon Manor had been completed (in 1881). Several houses were decoratively topped by the Rothschild crest of five arrows and a crown, symbolising the five fabulously successful brothers. There is a clock-tower here, a bit of Italianate late Victorian there, pseudo-Elizabethan chimneys, balconies, and other embellishments. Even when the house is closed to the public Waddesdon village is worth a stroll: there are antique shops, pubs, small hotels.

Some great houses benefit from a lived-in feeling but this is not one of Waddesdon's charms. It is a fabulous treasure house of near-priceless *objets d'art*, but these are, it has to be admitted, contained in a museum-like setting. In several rooms the drapes are permanently closed, so as not to spoil fabrics as fresh and pristine as the day they were installed. But for many visitors the best of Waddesdon is in the porcelain — rare Meissen and Sèvres, in rich aquamarine and turquoise so translucent you half believe it will glow in the dark. Among the interesting facts about the building of the house, for which a large slice of Lodge Hill was removed, is that the Bath stone from which it is largely constructed was transported from Quainton by a specially constructed steam railway.

The quickest return to Oxford is southwards via Ashendon or Long Crendon, Thame and the A40.

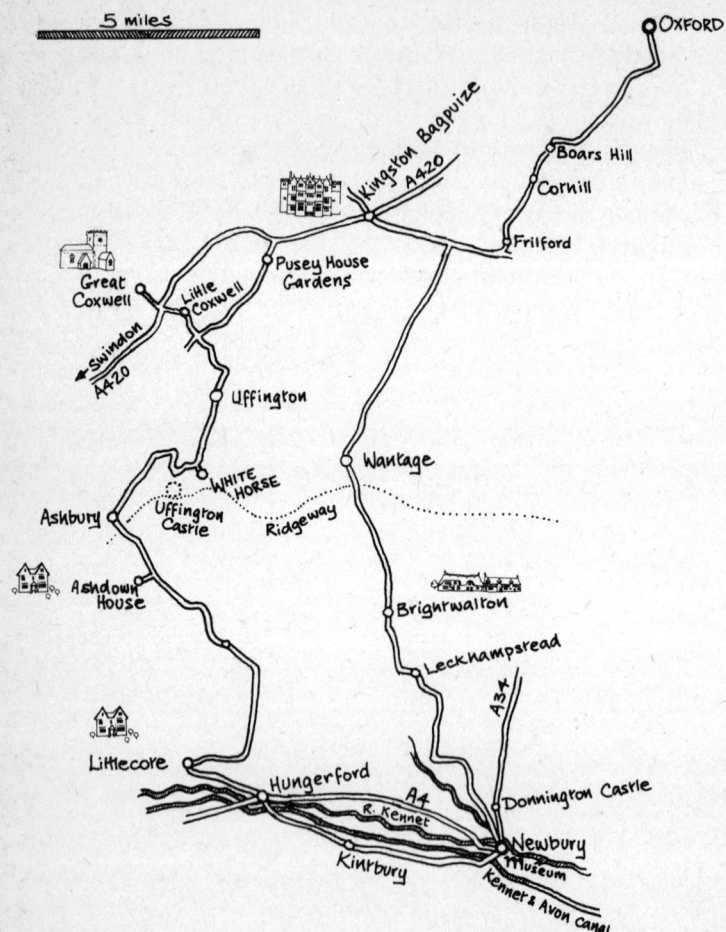

6 Vale of White Horse—Littlecote— Hungerford—Newbury (75-80 miles)

From Oxford pick up the A420 for Swindon, past Cumnor. The first port of call on this predominantly Berkshire Downs itinerary is the village of Kingston Bagpuize, which can be most swiftly reached on the A420, but far more prettily so by picking your way along lesser roads via Boars Hill, Wootton, Cothill and Frilford. You pass through attractive patches of matted woodlands and past many secluded houses.

Kingston House is easy to miss. Look for the sharp right-hand bend of the road as you enter the village, then follow the sign to Abingdon. The best first inspection of the house is from the back, along Rectory Lane—from the front it is largely hidden by trees. Neither the date of its construction nor the name of the architect are known, unusual for such a grandiose house, but it was certainly here in 1670.

Among the house's interior features is a magnificent cantilevered staircase and gallery, built without supporting pillars, its weight sustained by the walls. There are also Chinese handpainted wallpapers, fine oak panelling, furnishings and paintings, but in many ways it is the gardens that steal the limelight. The herbaceous and shrub borders, a profusion of bulbs, lawns and many rare trees are enclosed within a framework of mellow brick walls.

Pretty Pusey House Gardens lie just off the main A420 along a narrow road bordered by hedgerows. The house, a Georgian mansion, is not open to public scrutiny but the fifteen-acre gardens are. Midsummer is when the herbaceous borders and rose garden are at their most outstanding; autumn is ripe for trees in full flame, and early summer for the plants that both fringe and thrive in the lake. The garden sculptures, of course, look the same all the year round.

The name of the village is distinctive: it commemorates a William Pewse, who supposedly warned King Canute of a forthcoming ambush by the Saxons. In gratitude, Canute rewarded him with a gift of lands. The village church is of a simple, early 18th-century design with some spectacular stained glass windows, all memorials to the Pewse family.

Well worthwhile is a slight detour from the obvious route from Pusey to Fernham to see the Great Barn at Great Coxwell. Built in the 13th century by monks, the barn is a massive stone edifice, including a stone-tiled roof, shaped like a cross and held together by a maze of timbers that are in themselves a lesson in medieval architecture. It is undoubtedly one of the most impressive structures of its kind in Europe, as 'noble as a cathedral' according to William Morris, and still in use: the next-door farmer keeps his machinery, bags of chemicals and other agrarian bric-a-brac within its shelter. It is owned by the National Trust and open more or less always. But don't neglect the rest of the village, which is built mostly of now-weathered limestone with an old wizened church dating back to the 1200s, with a Jacobean pulpit.

Take the road back to Little Coxwell and on across the Vale of the White Horse, an all-revealing clue to the next point of interest. But before you reach the chalk downs you'll drive into Uffington. 'Tom Brown' spent his schooldays here, for Thomas Hughes was born here and made it the home of his hero—there's a memorial to the author in the 13th-century village church, which you can't miss on account of its highly unusual octagonal tower.

The change of flora that accompanies the climb on to the bare escarpment from the verdant pasture-lands below is almost as striking as going from jungle to desert. One minute you are engulfed by the cosiness of rural England, the next you begin to wonder if the search and rescue teams are on the alert, ready to find you if you should happen to stray from the road. But do stray from the road — or at least the White Horse car park.

This famous beast, 360 feet by 130 feet, has been galloping over these rolling Downs for many centuries. Most theories ascribe its origin to the Iron Age, perhaps as a cult figure tied to the worship of Epona, the Celtic goddess of horses. Other historians maintain that it was cut into the underlying chalk to commemorate King Alfred's victory over the Danes at nearby Ashdown in 871. Until the mid-19th century the scouring of the horse was an excuse for an important festival held every seventh year with eating, drinking, games, music and general merriment to accompany the more serious task of keeping the horse's outline clear. They would also have celebrated the demise of the 'dragon'. The detached lump of ground to the west and slightly below the line of the horse is known as Dragon's Hill, supposedly the spot where George slayed his beast. To prove the legend, you only have to look at the bare patch of earth where the grass refuses to grow on account of the blood that was spilled on it.

This corner of England is well endowed with prehistoric remains: Wayland's Smithy, a neolithic chambered tomb shown by excavation to date from 3500 BC, lies a mere one-and-a-half mile walk away. Its chambered bowels may be entered by anyone supple enough to bend beneath the hefty sandstone lintel. And Uffington Castle is one of the country's most famous Iron Age hill forts. Built in 500 BC — or even earlier — it consists of a single ditch, an inner bank and an outer strengthening bank, all spread over an eight-acre site on top of an 850-foot hill. Climb it and, on a clear day, you can see forever — well, at least as far as the outline of the Black Mountains of Wales.

Hill forts, according to the experts, may have served as tribal or cult centres, as markets and as a refuge in time of war. When Uffington was built, the line of the Downs was probably already in use as a trade route, for the Ridgeway is one of the country's, if not the world's, most ancient roads. In prehistoric times, when the surrounding lowlands were thick with forests and other vegetable matter, the chalk hills afforded a way of least resistance and one considerably drier than the boglands below. A Neolithic route once stretched all the way from the North Sea in East Anglia to the south-west coast at Devon, travelled by animal drovers and traders carrying flint weapons, stone implements, Irish gold, or amber from the Baltic countries.

The eighty-five miles that still remain of this original trackway have been designated as an official long-distance footpath. There are several 'feeder paths' to the Ridgeway in this area, all waymarked with CR plaques — Circular Routes — by Oxfordshire County Council.

After taking the bracing air of the Downs, you drive west on the B4507, parallel to the base of the escarpment, before turning south at Ashbury on the B4000, driving up and over the crest until you reach the rather bizarre-looking Ashdown House. It is a late 17th-century, four-storey affair, built out of chalk blocks and stone quoins, its mansard roof crowned by a green cupola and topped by a golden ball. In many ways it more closely resembles a monument or folly than a house, especially when viewed from the end of its long, tree-lined avenue. There are conducted tours to that fabulous roof.

Signs by the road warning motorists of the presence of galloping horses don't refer to chalk figures but to thoroughbred, and very much alive, animals. The Downs provide a vast training area for the racehorses of Lambourn and surrounding stables. The turf is both resilient and springy and a lucky sighting of animals galloping is not to be forgotten. But don't be disappointed if you fail to see any — on a recent visit the only horse I saw was an enormous dray being led along the road, so old he could barely manage a trot, let alone a gallop!

The village of Lambourn, with its Norman church and Victorian almshouses, was immortalised both as Maryland in Thomas Hardy's *Jude the Obscure* and described by Charles Kingsley in *Two Years Ago* under the name of Whitbury.

Littlecote lies almost due south of Lambourn, in the valley of the River Kennet, on the far side of the M4. Take the B4001 from Lambourn and turn right at the A419. It is best known for its Tudor manor house with fine panelling and plasterwork ceilings and a 17th-century armoury which includes Judge Popham's famous finger stocks, used at his Assizes to keep the prisoners quiet. The Long Gallery contains many antiques, and many of the bedrooms are decorated with exotic tapestries. There is also a resident ghost, harmless I'm told. Two even more surprising Littlecote attractions are an adjacent Roman Villa, still in the midst of excavation work and, even more remote, Frontier City, the name given to a programme of in-house (or in-grounds) authentic Wild West shows. All these sights, sounds and spectacles can be experienced on weekends and Bank Holiday afternoons from April until September.

Following the river downstream, you'll come to the small town of Hungerford, a veritable paradise for buyers of antiques and for dreamers too. An entire arcade and several scattered shops are exclusively devoted to selling all manner of objects from the past. Their combined effect is to make those more ordinary shops selling household goods, groceries and electrical appliances seem very banal indeed. Even more human aspects of Hungerford life are coated in history. It has, for example, neither a mayor nor corporation; Hungerford's senior citizen is called the Constable and he is assisted by a Portreeve, a Bailiff and a court of 12 Feoffees. On the second Tuesday after Easter officers are elected at the colourful Court Leet ceremony.

The Kennet and Avon canal which flows past the town affords both a lovely setting and lots of towpath leg-stretching. It was open for business in 1810, flowing from the Avon at Bristol into the Thames at Reading, and was one of only two broad canals across England south of the Pennines. As a vital artery in the Victorian communications network it was, in its heyday, hectic with barges — although when seen in the light of today's tranquillity it is hard to imagine such commercial purposes.

Follow the line of the canal either along the eastbound A4 or the gentler route to the south via Kintbury and you'll quickly reach Newbury. Although the training of horses may be a Down-based activity, the principal racecourse in the area is here, and meetings are held from time to time throughout the year. A thriving, prosperous town in the Middle Ages, Newbury's history is most succinctly revealed in its museum, housed in the 17th-century Cloth Hall on Wharf Street. Along with the story behind the town's two Civil War battles, you'll find other exhibits devoted to a motley range of subjects from flint tools to old-fashioned cameras.

The Kennet at Newbury

You can both stroll along the towpath or be carried by horse-drawn barge (in July and August at least). Stop by the parish church of St Nicholas, built by 'Jack of Newbury', alias John Smalwoode who was once the most important clothier in the country, a fearless soldier (he led a small contingent of men against the Scots in the battle of Flodden) and friend of kings: Henry VIII stayed in his house in Northbrooke Street, now alas in ruins.

Just to the north of town, on the homeward leg to Oxford, just off the B4494, are the remains of Donnington Castle. Built in the 14th century, the castle did not make headline news until the Civil War, when it was twice beseiged by Cromwell, the latter struggle lasting nearly two years. Only two round towers, the old gateway and the three-storeyed gatehouse are still standing, the latter containing a collection of bullets, cannonballs and shell fired by the Parliamentarians.

If time allows, a far more attractive route back to Oxford than the A34 will carry you through a series of Berkshire's little-known villages, including Leckhamstead, high on the Downs, with its curious church, and Brightwalton (a collection of thatched cottages surrounded by hills and typical Downland beechwoods), as well as the busier market town of Wantage situated on the old Roman road that crosses the Downs. This was the birthplace of King Alfred, who was largely responsible for the poor reputation of Britain's food.

7 Abingdon – Didcot – Dorchester – Thame (60 miles)

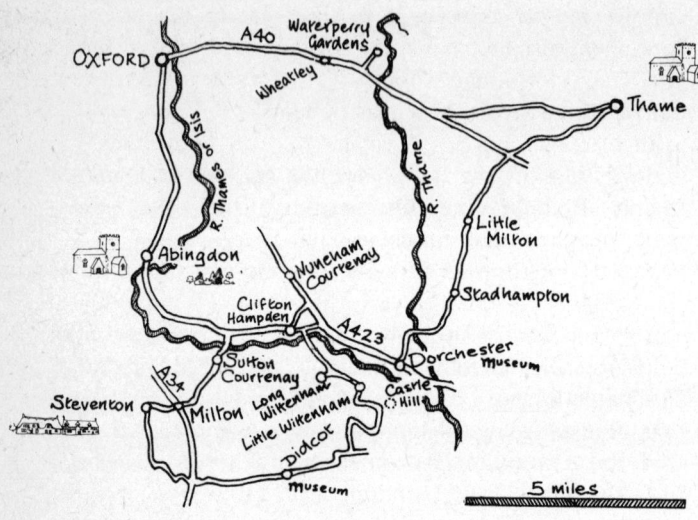

To get quickly under way on this route, simply pick up signs for the A34 for Abingdon, due south of Oxford. Oxford's road system may seem tortuous but signs are good and the one-way schemes efficient. Abingdon is just a few minutes' drive. Although most famous for being the town that built MG sports cars, the town has quite a history in its own right. Founded by monks on the confluence of the River Ock and the River Thames some nine hundred years ago, Abingdon grew to become a prosperous market town. When its Benedictine abbey, part of which still remains, was dissolved by Henry VIII in 1538, it was the sixth richest in Britain and one of the country's most important religious houses.

The Abbey is still the town's star attraction, though its remaining parts now occupy a tiny proportion of the original site, a vast complex of buildings and grounds. As you drive into the town from Oxford the Old Abbey Gateway stands to your left. Park and wander through, past the 12th-century church of St Nicholas and various offices belonging to the local borough, and turn down Checker Walk. At the end of this pleasant street you'll find the Abbey Granary, the Checker — a fine 13th-century building — and the Long Gallery, with its magnificent beamed roof. All are open to the public.

In the heart of Abingdon's market square is the 17th-century County Hall. The ground-floor level is an open area and still serves its original purpose as a shelter for market traders: the market is held every Monday, while the upper floor, which used to be the court room, is now the town's museum. Opposite St Nicholas's Church, and linked by the Abbey Gatehouse, is the Guildhall, accompanied by medieval buildings, including the Crown and Thistle, an old coaching inn. There is also Berkshire's old County Gaol, built by Napoleonic prisoners of war and now an excellent arts and leisure centre.

The river at Abingdon moves gracefully past the town. It can be enjoyed at first hand from a boat (easily hired from the boatyards by the bridge) or you can just idly watch its progress from the Nag's Head pub or The Upper Reaches hotel, built on the site of a monastic watermill. The bridge, wider than it is long, was built in 1416 by the Guild of the Fraternity of the Holy Cross, now Christ's Hospital, and was rebuilt in 1928-9. It is your way out of town and on across the broad Thames Valley.

A couple of miles outside Abingdon, following the A415 to Henley, turn right for Sutton Courtenay by the Wagon and Horses pub. But we recommend a detour for rose lovers, who should first carry on to Nuneham Courtenay (turn left, about four miles further along the Henley road, then join the A423 from the B4015). It is home to the John Mattock Rose

Abingdon

Nurseries where, at their prime in June, July and August, there are some 300,000 roses of various varieties to be admired. There's also a plant information centre where you can learn all about 'rose technology', and if you happen to be passing on a Saturday in early March, you can take a lesson in pruning.

Meanwhile, back at the Sutton Courtenay turning, you will see the Didcot power station. Try to ignore it! The approach rows of houses to Sutton Courtenay are also unpromising but your patience will be rewarded by some later delightful buildings, many of which abut on to the classic village green. There's a fine walk to be savoured too, alongside the Sutton Pools, no doubt once enjoyed by Eric Blair, better known as

George Orwell, who lies buried in the churchyard, and David Astor, former owner of the *Observer*, who lives here.

Continue via the B4016 and the B4017 on to Steventon, which will involve a slight but obvious detour for the sake of a number of timber-framed 13th- and 14th-century National Trust cottages. They stand alongside the ancient tree-lined, stone-paved Causeway which, in days before the Vale was properly drained, often afforded the only dry thoroughfare.

In fact, if you leave your car near the village war memorial and walk along it, you'll find the first group of cottages on the near side of the co-op, the second just after the road twists (to the right, then left) and a third beyond the railway.

In this busy corner of the county, it's not always easy to come across such a peaceful backwater as Milton Manor House, which brings a feeling of blissful relief. Sir John Betjeman must have felt the same way about Milton when he wrote 'Like all the best things in England this is hidden. The Manor House is splendid.' Inigo Jones is thought to have designed the building. William of Orange stayed here when he came to England to be crowned. It is modest in scale but its Georgian wings, a chapel and library built in 'Strawberry Hill Gothic', extend its proportions. Among its motley treasures is a collection of 200 teapots.

Didcot is not a lovely place, but they have to put power stations somewhere. The main source of interest for the casual visitor is in a different sort of power, however. For an impressive collection of locos, rolling stock and other railway hardware, including its most prized exhibit, the *Shannon*, the world's oldest standard-gauge loco still in working order, is housed in the Didcot Railway Centre, a depot by the town's railway station.

Didcot is a fitting place indeed for such a major train museum. It was once a sleepy village that, in 1841, awoke to find that Brunel had brought the Great Western Railway to town, transforming it into a vital railway junction.

From Didcot you pass into open countryside again. The road climbs and soon reveals two isolated humps of ground, each crowded with beech trees. For a more intimate contact follow the signs to Long Wittenham along a narrow windswept road lined with well-groomed hedges and, at its junction with a mainish route, follow the signs to Little Wittenham up a steeply banked and twisting road.

There is a small car park below the twin hills of Sinodun, known locally as Wittenham Clumps, and especially if you have your wellies handy you should climb to the top of the nearest, Castle Hill, to enjoy an amazing view of such pastoral charms as the distant Chilterns and the broad Thames Valley. This hill is also of interest as the site of an Iron Age hill fort, with a clearly defined ditch and bank to prove it. On a windy day the noise from the summit is like a wide-bodied aircraft taking off at Heathrow. But don't be tempted to bring your hang glider — a notice by the car park strictly forbids it.

Save time for a lengthy pause at Little Wittenham village, a very pretty collection of cottages and an even prettier church, all of which stand at the end of an 'access only' road and so remain unmolested by all but the most determined visitors. Then, if you don't feel you've already had an overdose of trains, call in at the Pendon Museum in the neighbouring village of Long Wittenham (the reason it is 'long' as opposed to 'little' will be obvious as soon as you cruise along its main street). The museum, run entirely by volunteers, is at the far end of the village. Pendon Museum houses a collection of model railways but that, in itself, is far too narrow a definition. It is really an amazing portrait in miniature of the Vale of the White Horse (Dartmoor landscapes are featured too), specifically rooted in the 1930s, and as much importance is put upon the rural scene as the trains themselves. The painstaking craftsmanship throughout is admirable.

If you have a good excuse — you are passing at lunchtime,

say—stop at the Barley Mow at Clifton Hampden. This 14th-century half-timbered, white and 'cruck'-walled inn, with distinctive low-pitched gables, a thatched roof and latticed windows, is 'without exception . . . the quaintest, most old-world inn up the river'. So wrote Jerome K. Jerome in *Three Men in a Boat*. If you stand anything above five foot six inches in your Wittenham Clump mud-spattered shoes, be sure to keep your head down—the Barley beams are the lowest imaginable.

Follow the short stretch of main road, by no means an unappealing drive, to Dorchester. Here was a city in ancient British times, being known as Caer Doren, the 'city on the water' on account of its position on one of the principal Thames tributaries. In Roman times it was the capital of Wessex and the Venerable Bede recorded that it was a 'cathedral city' which explains why its church is so high and mighty.

The Abbey Church of St Peter and St Paul was founded by Augustinian Canons around 1140 on the site of a former Saxon cathedral, but the building as seen today stems largely from the 13th and 14th centuries. It is especially revered for its Norman lead font and brilliant stained glass windows and fine tracery, much of it restored as a memorial to Sir Winston Churchill in 1966. The abbey has a museum, housed in the monastery guest house (the only monastic building to survive the Dissolution of 1536), a cloister garden and archives that date the town's existence to a continuous settlement since 2500 BC.

The church tower dominates the town's timbered and thatched houses, its shops (especially antiques) and some fine old inns, including the George Hotel, opposite the abbey's Victorian lychgate with its galleried courtyard and a 19th-century yellow stage-coach (minus the horses) which you'll see permanently moored outside.

Most of the town's inns date back to the 17th and 18th

centuries, when the town was a key stage-coach stop on the London to Oxford road. Save time, pubs aside, for a substantial stroll around the town's smaller lanes, alleyways and paths that lie off and behind the main street.

Across yet another bridge and then briefly on to the Dorchester bypass before taking the road to Thame via Stadhampton and Little Milton: this is the longest stretch of rural riding in the day's itinerary, with plenty of ups and downs to give good en-route vantage points across the farmland scenery. The sights vary between meadowland and pig farm, edible crops and a windmill, while in the distance there is the constant companionship of the Chilterns.

Before you drive into the heart of Thame stop to look at its church. Dating from the 1240s this mere parish church of St Mary's looks like a miniature cathedral. It is so rich in historic brasses that brass rubbers now have to make a special appointment with the vicar before being allowed to set about their work.

Thame is a now familiar scene of lovely half-timbered buildings or, more commonly, Georgian façades, topped by the occasional thatched roof. At its core is the market square . . . or rather diagonal, boundaried by the Buttermarket and Cornmarket streets and cleaved by Thame's Victorian Town Hall (where you'll find the Tourist Information Centre) and other buildings. Tuesday is market day in Thame, just as it has been since 1183.

If you thought Dorchester was well endowed with inns just wait till you cast your eye over Thame's old faithfuls. The Birdcage in Cornmarket, with its oriel windows and over-hanging upper storey, is probably the oldest (its cellar is supposedly 13th-century, although the main structure is more youthful — circa 1400).

In Buttermarket the most senior is the Saracen's Head, again with an ancient cellar. Thame is good for shopping in a style that used to be widespread before the high streets all began to look alike. There are some chain-store fronts, of course, but somehow the atmosphere is timeless.

A final stop before heading back to Oxford via the A40 could well be Waterperry Gardens. Bordering the river Thame just before Wheatley, these peaceful gardens, surrounding an 18th-century manor house, were a well-known horticultural school up until the early 1970s. Fine herbaceous borders, a fruit garden, glasshouses and an alpine nursery are still in evidence (though the house itself is not open to the public). Pop into the village's ivy-covered church, too, to see the high box-pews which are still lit by candles, and some exceptional stained-glass windows.

The exact routes described in this book may not suit everyone exactly, and in order to make them more flexible we have devised alternative journeys that take in what are, to our mind, the 'essential' points of interest around Oxford. We have not accompanied them with maps, as we have avoided all but essential minor or unclassified roads.

A.   East of Oxford

A taste of rural Northamptonshire is a must, and we recommend driving almost due north towards Sulgrave, even by the rather functional A423. Just south of there, though it does not figure in one of the more detailed itineraries in the book, is Brackley, a very good place for everyday shopping as well as browsing among antique shops and just enjoying the unusually wide main street. South of Brackley (via the A43 is quickest) lies Bicester, from where Waddesdon and spectacular Waddesdon Manor can be visited: take the A41. The market town of Thame would be well within the scope of a busy day trip and so would Dorchester-on-Thames — never, incidentally, to be confused with the principal town of Dorset. On your return to Oxford from Dorchester it would be hard to miss Abingdon. Not unduly upset by its transfer years ago from Berkshire to Oxfordshire, it is a pleasant, spacious historic town.

B.   West of Oxford

It is possible, by judicious timing, to experience both the taste of the windswept downs, trodden by prehistoric man, and the neat, cosy enclaves of the Cotswolds proper. Drive to Abingdon, then to Uffington, above which looms White Horse Hill. From Uffington go due north towards Faringdon and Lechlade, then to Burford. This is one of five or six Cotswold towns that should not be missed. The others lie, conveniently, almost due north: Bourton-on-the-Water, Stow-on-the-Wold, Moreton-in-Marsh, Broadway, Chipping Campden. And if you should have time to see, on your way back to Oxford, something of The Tews (Great Tew is best, and lies just a few miles off the fast A34) then so much the better.